# LEADERSHIP TACTICS

## EVERYDAY MILITARY WISDOM

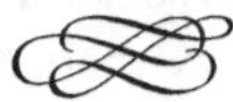

## BRANDON SIMPSON

# CONTENTS

# INTRODUCTION

Would you like to become a leader? This is one of those rare books which will shine light on how to become a true, successful, and accomplished leader, drawing lessons from how it is taught and practiced in the military. Every chapter can guide you on how leadership can be applied to everyday life—both personal and professional—transforming your everyday challenges into wonderful opportunities for success.

## LEADERSHIP CAN BE EMULATED

Before we begin, I'd like to share a secret with you that will empower you on your journey to becoming a confident leader.

In this world, we have such amazing examples of leadership —some are presidents in our world history who brought beneficial changes to their countries and the world, some are CEOs of major successful companies, some are revolutionaries who freed their countries from oppression and colonial control, and others are generals and soldiers who fought bravely to win wars. One might feel their victories are incomprehensible, events that cannot be repeated or emulated easily. Successes of these grand proportions may intimidate us. The very experiences may seem out of reach. In my experience, however, and the testimonies shared by some of the major influential military figures of all time, it is possible to learn the secrets behind such successful leadership and be able to do it again, so to speak.

## THE PRINCIPLES OF TEAM WORK, GENIUS, AND A COURAGEOUS SPIRIT

During the Middle Ages, a battle was fought between the peasantry and their aristocratic overlords. The noblemen came to battle on horses, all armed with weapons, with armor for their protection. The weaker party, namely, the peasants, had only scythes and pitchforks as weapons. Any historian knowing only these as the facts could have proceeded to announce that the noblemen must have won the battle; it was the peasants, however, who won! Their leadership figures brought strategic thinking, teamwork, and resourcefulness to the battle. What they did was this—on the eve of battle, they flooded the battlefield by channeling the waters of a nearby river. Since it was the thick of winter, the water froze overnight. In the morning, when the noblemen proceeded to cross the battlefield on their horses, they found their horses slipping and falling. The peasants, who in the meantime had prepared themselves for walking on ice, came to the battlefield with whatever they had and easily defeated their overlords.

Battles like this have occurred over thousands of years, each battle with its own unique story. The details regarding which side won and on what dates always make it to the textbooks in our classrooms. But the little-known reasons for victory often remain hidden. Army generals, and leaders, and how they governed their battalions before battle and in the thick of battle, are the real reason behind the victories we only know the dates of. Great generals and leaders have been known to inspire their men, women, and people with great zeal and heroic strength. It is this kind of leadership that succeeds in the face of seemingly undefeatable odds or an enemy who is superior in weaponry. Good military leadership, which is a unique blend of practical brilliance and inspiration, has led many countries to victory.

## THE UNIVERSALITY OF LEADERSHIP

Any difficult principle or tactic applied by a knowledgeable and naturally confident leader can be applied by you too in the contexts and situations life presents to you. The rule is simple—if you understand it well enough in common everyday contexts, and can practice the idea behind the tactic, you will develop it as a muscle memory and can practice it in any kind of situation. Know that deep understanding, once achieved in one context, will kick into action in a new, uncharted, or much more complex situation as well. The following story will demonstrate this point, in addition to introducing the concept that leadership skills are accessible to anyone who puts their mind and heart into them.

## WISDOM FROM THE VOICES OF MILITARY LEADERSHIP

Compiled in this book, you will find wisdom from a military style of leadership which I gathered from my own life experience in the Texas State Guard, and also from figures like Simon Sinek, author of 'Start with Why', Col. Dandridge Malone, Navy Admiral William H. McRaven, Statesman General Collin Powell, Ex-US Navy Seal Jocko Willink, Ex-US Navy Seal Leif Babin, Ex-US Navy Seal David Goggins, and acclaimed author J. Donald Walters, who had spent time studying the military and is known for his book 'Art of Supportive Leadership' (among other books) which is currently used as one of the training guides for the US armed forces. We're going to be exploring just how wisdom nurtured in the military, and insights on military leadership can apply to your life and change it for the better.

No matter your race, ethnicity, gender, sexual orientation, financial status, religion, or physical or mental capability, this book is for you if you are willing to aim for your own highest potential to unfold in life. This book requires readers to adopt an attitude of courage, adaptability, and bravado. It will offer simple exercises, but they do need you to let go of fears and try these new techniques. If you've been used to egoic biases, you'll need to start letting them go. This work is made for you to find the answers to not just solving the daily life challenges, but also seeing each one as an opportunity for creating unbeatable grand successes in the short term, and more so in the long term.

Through these time-tested military leadership principles, you can improve yourself and deliver a constructive and lasting impact among your friends, colleagues, and even enemies and adversaries.

## THE LAYOUT OF THE BOOK

The first three chapters of the book focus on some of the foundations and basic principles involved in becoming a leader, whether that is in the military, any organization, or in your personal endeavors and relationships.

Hierarchy, teamwork, collaboration, and the full implications of responsibility are dealt with in the next three chapters. Here you will learn how leadership and these necessary aspects of practicing true leadership are essential for efficiency in your dealings with others.

The final two chapters talk about the importance of diplomacy for a leader or for anyone practicing leadership principles in their life. It is the ultimate tool for escaping troubles and rising to unheard-of success. Discussed is also the relation between freedom and power, both of which are concepts usually associated with each other, though misunderstood in regards to what the relationship really entails. In these last two chapters, you can learn how freedom and power are often related, and more importantly, how they need to be adopted in the right way for your leadership to be a real success.

Additionally, toward the end of every chapter, practical steps for the application of leadership skills are mentioned to help you take these pearls of wisdom forward in your life. In some of the chapters, talks by military and leadership figures have been included.

The conclusion of the book will have a self-assessment exercise that will help you take charge of any situation in life. It will help you have a successful and innovative leadership practice in your personal and professional life.

# FOUNDATIONS OF MILITARY LEADERSHIP

*"Leadership requires openness to the feelings of others, and not insensitivity to them in the name of 'getting on with the job.' To a major extent, their welfare is the job."*

— J. DONALD WALTERS

## LEADERSHIP TRAITS AND PRINCIPLES OVERVIEW

Ten main principles of leadership which are practiced in the US Armed Forces, and sixteen time-honored traits that are known to be important for true leadership, have been taught by a well-known and renowned US Army colonel named Col. Dandridge M. Malone. Colonel Malone served in the US Army for several decades and taught these principles and traits to soldiers in training. They've been paraphrased here:

### Military Leadership Principles

- Understanding your own self better and improving yourself.
- Being knowledgeable about techniques, tactics, and strategies.
- Being prompt about undertaking and meeting responsibilities.
- Making decisions that are smart and time-sensitive.
- Inspiring others by leading with your own example.
- Getting to know your soldiers/team and having their welfare in mind.
- Keeping your soldiers/team in the loop about the mission at all times.
- Helping lower ranks and subordinates develop their leadership skills.
- Overseeing the accomplishment of tasks.
- Develop team spirit among your soldiers/team members.

### Sixteen Important Leadership Traits

If you are striving to be a leader in your personal or professional life, the following are important qualities to develop. How these can be practically applied will be discussed in detail in the following chapters.

| | | | |
|---|---|---|---|
| • Courage | • Bearing | • Loyalty | • Endurance |
| • Enthusiasm | • Humility | • Initiative | • Integrity |
| • Judgment | • Justice | • Tact | • Dependability |
| • Selflessness | • Knowledge | • Humor | • Decisiveness |

These principles and traits are very relevant to all aspects of one's life. That is right—they are not just meant to be practiced on the battlefield.

Examples:

- When we are aware that someone less privileged than us needs someone to speak for them, or on their behalf, so that they are represented well and are heard, it requires **initiative.** This quality is an important one practiced by military members for military purposes, and people can develop initiative skills in a lot of ways. Another opportunity to develop it is when you feel something needs to happen or change in the world—you can go ahead and **initiate** the change yourself. Be the first one!
- Wise **judgment** and **tact** are needed for a lot of things, and requires a certain detachment and skill of looking at situations in life objectively. For example, when answering a salesman you're going to say no to, the need is to see the offer objectively and make a judgment about buying, but the need is also to speak politely and tactfully when turning down the offer.
- When we practice friendship, **humor**, and **humility** will bring grace into the sourest or bitterest of moments, often saving friendships from getting destroyed.
- **Selflessness**, another one of the traits of a good military leader, when practiced in friendships, is what draws to us true friends as opposed to false or superficial friends.

- When our **integrity** and **loyalty** are questioned or tested, we can especially focus on being true to the ones who have loved us and supported us in doing good in this world. A higher octave than that also exists and that is when everyone we know misunderstands us, and those who were once close to turn against us, we can turn to our own inner conscience and strive to remain loyal to that voice. In time, one's integrity, if we have practiced it throughout, will be proven in the eyes of others as well. This is an essential reason why doing the right thing, even when others aren't looking, is important.

## LEADERSHIP TRAITS AND PRINCIPLES IN ACTION

### *Leadership Principles in Action in the Professional Life*

How military leadership principles mentioned above play out in a variety of professions, and scenarios—right from schools to governments, corporate offices to private businesses, projects collaborated upon to private independent single-individual ventures like freelancing. Here are real-world examples of successful applications:

- **How you assess yourself and perform:** Students normally are assessed by teachers. But if they have a way to self-assess, they can keep track of developing their own selves and aiming for higher capacities from a young age. Self-assessment tools are handy, not just when they reach the stage of taking their SATs, but also throughout the schooling years right from the start. The Living Wisdom Schools in the US and Italy are a good example of schools that nurture such leadership in children.

- **How you motivate yourself:** This is a key area where your ability to lead your life by very good standards is judged. Ultimately, the standard we set for ourselves is the standard that's really going to matter. Anyone else out there setting standards may change them at any time—many people are shifty, and it's just human nature that most people change their expectations and standards easily over time. But that shouldn't deter us from meeting our highest potential. We need to set our own standards in life and live up to them. One place where motivation gets tested is any private venture like a family business or independent business. Leadership is required to run it, and it wouldn't happen without a good deal of daily motivation. One simple answer— love yourself, dedicate your efforts to the ones you love, and make excellent service the goal.

- **Being knowledgeable about techniques, strategies, and tactics:** In any work or professional service you do, some basic research in the field/subject/industry is required, if not some thorough research. Knowing some of its history, its challenges, its accomplishments, and its goals moving into the future leads to the tools, tactics, and techniques you need (the 3 T's) to then overcome the challenges and meet the needs of your customer/client/work in this profession.

- **Using acceptance of your imperfect reality, or a difficult situation, to keep getting better:** Whenever you want to be freed of some weakness, imperfection, flaw in yourself, or problem, first always face it fearlessly and then accept it completely. When humility sets in, it's time to start thinking about how you're going to "transcend" the challenge. Statesman General Collin Powell demonstrates this habit in his profession very well.
- **What do you do when you find a competitor stronger than you?** This is the situation where you can think of it as competing against your own past performance rather than thinking you are competing against others. In the end analysis, you can only improve your own self by changing something in your own functioning. While you may get ideas about wanting to be the best, be better, etc. one's goal in life, practically speaking, comes down to bringing out the best from within you. If jealousy overpowers you, you won't be able to think creatively about being successful. A charitable attitude is essential, part of which is accepting others' right to make their own place in the world.

*Leadership Principles in Action for Personal Growth*

## Health and Healing

Making decisions (that are smart and time-sensitive) is important for everyone, not just fighter pilots and the military. In life, there is a lot to do with timing. While undue pressure is one thing, a natural unfoldment of a life process, or someone having a certain need at a given time, makes it important to fulfill those needs in a timely manner. Eating three meals a day, for example, and making sure you prepare them on time or get them available for yourself and your family is very important. Time management comes in handy here. College-goers may not feel so bound by the regularity needed in having three proper meals every day, but soon all students and youngsters realize how important one's health and its demands are. Nurturing the body is the foundation on which you build your life.

## Relationships

Conjugal, friendly, and the familial. Challenges come in many shades. Let's consider two extremes: When we feel the pain of rejection or betrayal by loved ones, and when everything is going so well, that we want to be able to do more for the ones we love.

- When tough times come to us in relationships, our power of **endurance** and **knowledge** get tested. We need to especially act **dependably** in those times, rather than giving up, for the sake of our families, or for the sake of one's own duty in life, one's dreams and purpose in life; we need to choose triumph over hardships. Hardships come for this reason alone—to make us stronger. It's when our willpower gets tested.
- When we need energy and we sincerely want to feel energized for the sake of enjoying company, family, and friends, that is a time when we can practice **enthusiasm**. It is said that if you want to be enthusiastic, all you have to do is *act* enthusiastic.

- Helping someone out because you care for them, not because you want something in return. This requires **courage**, and to let go of selfish interests. Another side of this coin is trying to help others even when they want something of a selfish interest fulfilled through you—in those times, you can still help them (not in the way they want, but in a way you deem right for them) by being impersonal, not cold, and practicing **tact**.

## Financial Progress and Career Growth

You can aim high and achieve your ambitious financial targets/career dreams with military leadership in action. For example, rather than competing with others, and thinking just about making money from customers, think about making your customers truly happy. This service-oriented and gracious attitude, which is especially practiced by military members, can take you on the most successful journey in your business and profession.

## Educational Goals

Military leadership principles will be put to the test, especially when you complete college education and look for your first job. The world will seem like a war zone, and competition will seem tough. If you're not one of the high scorers of the class, and many times, even if you are, you'll still need to prove yourself, be clear and consistent about what your goals are, and be ready to do the most basic lower tier jobs in the company of your choice if you truly want to be employed and start somewhere. Gratitude for a simple job may not come easy, but in the long run, it will pay huge dividends and take you to great heights.

## Relating to Children

You can practice leadership with children while also instilling this very important quality in them. Their lives will be a lot more blessed if they learn early on to take initiative and make a habit of leading and disciplining their own energies. You can model this quality of being in charge of your energy/mood/behavior to them, and can even inspire them through stories, songs, and games. Soon children too will learn this important military leadership skill of being in charge of their own selves at all times. A good book on the subject is *Education for Life* by J. Donald Walters.

### *A Leadership Success Story Employing Military Leadership*

David Goggins, an ex-Navy SEAL, through his varied life experiences right from childhood, gained important insights about life and leading life. As a young African American boy, he faced many challenges, such as parental conflict at home, racism, poverty, obesity, a congenital heart condition, and a learning disorder. His aim, desire, and motivation throughout was to overcome the challenges, along with his mother, and achieve one of the hardest goals to achieve—becoming a Navy Seal and an athlete.

Let's identify five key takeaways from this story—qualities exercised or leadership principles put into action:

- "Don't focus on what you think you deserve; take aim at what you are willing to earn."—in David Goggins's own words. When anything you thought you deserved is missing or taken away, do something to earn it rather than expect it to be given without any effort on your part.
- Never blame your background or challenges for any weakness or lack of ambition in yourself. Ambition is for everyone. Choosing to be ambitious comes with needing to overcome every obstacle in your life.
- Any ambition one chooses needs to be seen and held as "achievable" by you, not as something too high, as wishful thinking, or something you won't take seriously enough.

## ADAPTING MILITARY LEADERSHIP TO DAILY LIFE

***Strategies Translating Military Leadership into Practical Habits***

Leadership traits in everyday life—what does it look like in daily common everyday activities/interactions/habits? This is basically the personal arena. We read about leaders and their personal lives in stories or novels sometimes; we even watch inspiring movies about them. But what would it mean to practice these traits when we are not leading lives as officially appointed leaders? Can we learn to develop these very same qualities and habits? How would it benefit us? What would it look like? Also, how do we draw important lessons from what happens on the battlefield when we hear stories of bravery, courage, and tactical brilliance?

Some basic strategies:

- **Independence in thought, action, and feeling**: Creating your own destiny with these qualities.
- **Viewing the world around you as your team:** Seeing the human race, your family, friends, and community as extensions of your own self and as teammates in the mission concerning your life and their lives.
- **Overseeing the development and welfare of your teammates:** First, adopt the path of wisdom in life—leadership involves practicing wisdom. Then, you may develop the ability to identify those who seem to be coming from immature desires, or those still on the way to maturity; at other times, even those way ahead of you in age may seem less mature than you. In every case where you sense a lack of wisdom, accept your role first in being the leader/guide in charge of your own life. Don't get swept by the opinions and suggestions of those being ruled by their desires/weaknesses. Following this habit, you can start to offer to these people in your life as much of a voice of truth (wisdom) as they are open to hearing—the truths that are for their own welfare.

- **Developing your powers of knowledge and concentration:** Gear your daily life, as simple as it may seem, toward developing your concentration powers, as well as your knowledge—both about yourself and the world.
- **Creating a vision for your life:** Leaders are not born with visions; they create a vision, and then they enter it and live it to the fullest. It can be a simple vision, easy to achieve, or it could be a very ambitious vision; either way, have an expansive vision for your life and your path.

*Personal Anecdote by 1st Lieutenant Brandon Simpson (Author)*

My personal motivation lies in selfless service. I joined the Texas State Guard with the intention of contributing to a greater cause beyond my individual interests. Recognizing the potential to positively impact others' lives, I embraced this opportunity to transcend personal complacency and dedicate myself to meaningful pursuits.

The evolution I experienced was straightforward: I engaged in activities that supported my state and fellow citizens and derived fulfillment and enjoyment from the process. While some may call me a "weekend warrior," my commitment extends beyond the confines of uniformed service. My goal always is to remain steadfast in assisting my community and fellow Texans.

Additionally, I recognize the importance of serving as a role model for my daughter, friends, and family. Through my actions and dedication to honorable conduct, I aspire to inspire those around me to pursue their own paths with integrity and purpose.

### *Simple Words of Wisdom—Deep and Multiple Shades of Meaning*

*"Great leaders are willing to sacrifice personal interests for the good of the team."*

—JOHN C. MAXWELL

- **Sacrificing personal interests when necessary, but don't compromise on principles:** While you sacrifice your personal interests in the process of your team's welfare, do not compromise on principles you hold dear—values and tenets you choose to live by. That is personal to you, but those are abstract guidelines that guide you in your life. Don't let go of those.
- **Greatness—in action, not for recognition:** Aim for that greatness, not so you get recognized, but so that your actions speak 'greatness'. They say actions speak louder than words. Think deeply about what that means. Greatness in the tasks you accomplish can inspire people in a variety of ways. Greatness shouldn't be aimed for if you want others to utter flattering comments about you.
- **Examples:** Joan of Arc is a famous example from history who led France to victory. She gave up her simple country maiden's country life in order to fight with men and soldiers and lead her nation to victory against England at Orleans. Mahatma Gandhi is

another great example of leadership who led his country to freedom on the strength of the discipline he developed every day since his education began. He let go of a lot of personal comforts for the sake of the rest of his countrymen, especially for setting a high example so that youngsters would find it inspiring to follow him in freeing India. There are many other such people who have chosen greatness in action for the good of the team/their country.

## PRACTICAL EXERCISE

- Can leadership be applied in such a way that it promotes mental health? Watch the following video by a leading expert on mental health and leadership:

- What personal interests are you willing to let go of this year for the welfare of others who you care about, and for those you view as your teammates in the battle of life? Journal in a small diary and discuss with a friend this leadership trait.

## CONCLUSION

In the next chapter, we will learn the importance of bringing compassionate discipline, rigor, and regularity to the practice of these high principles taught in this chapter. Nothing substantial or powerful was ever achieved without the powers of concentration, clarity, accountability, and discipline; hence we move on now to understand how to bring these into daily life situations to ensure efficiency and solidity.

# DISCIPLINE AND ACCOUNTABILITY

*"It is not only what we do, but also what we do not do, for which we are accountable."*

— MOLIERE

## MILITARY DISCIPLINE AND PERSONAL GROWTH

Bertram I. Spector, in his report called *Military Self-Discipline: A Motivational Analysis* writes (1978):

The traditional concept of military-style discipline involves a rigid and unquestioning adherence to rules, commands, authority, and subordination.... military authority is gradually shifting from this traditional concept of absolute discipline to a more flexible and "positive" form of discipline.... judgment and improvisation are becoming more critical to successful performance than strict adherence to rigid rules. (p. 2, p.3)

## *The Role of Discipline in Military Training*

- **Developing the ability to endure pain/being tough**:
The military teaches how to become tough through
the practice of discipline. It's one sector where
beauty sleep is not an option—it's the vocation of
early risers, whether they enjoy the early rise
discipline or not at first. The tough part is going
through training that is really difficult on the body,
causes hurts and wounds, and tests strength,
endurance, flexibility, patience, tenacity, and a whole
lot of other things. One learns not to take the body
so seriously, or its comfort and perfection so
seriously.

- **The soldier's readiness to sacrifice her or his life
in battle/emergencies:** This is one of the very noble
and heroic qualities of a leader, soldier, or one who is
out there to serve their fellowmen in an ultimate
sense—they love others even more than themselves.
The life of a fellow soldier, or the life of one needing
rescue during a natural disaster, is more precious to
military leaders than their own lives. They are true
warriors. But this ability is not one shown recklessly.
It is employed with tact, skill, and disciplined control
over oneself, such that the other person survives the
difficulty.

- **Overcoming fear/restlessness/nervousness and
cowardice:** The role of discipline in the military is to
help you transcend these obstacles. While it is
natural to feel these qualities, it is special when one
overcomes them with the use of powerful habits and
discipline. Being in the military can help you

overcome these obstacles, even if it is only for a certain amount of time. It trains one for the long run to live a successful and strong life.

- **Discipline in the military teaches that discipline needs to come from within:** Once you learn to love discipline, it starts to come from within rather than you needing it imposed or being taught to you from outside.

- **Discipline of the body is great, but discipline of the mind is far greater:** One learns this nowhere better than in the military. Disciplining both are important. In a way, when you work on your mind, your body also becomes stronger. And when you work on your body, strengthening it also strengthens the mind. Great feats have been achieved based on this truth. However, in the end analysis, the mind, thoughts, and the heart's feelings—all of which are connected, are there for us to be able to experience the higher things in life. Disciplining these so that they can tune into the joy and bliss of the soul is important and the hardest thing of all.

### *Narrative: Personal Development Through Disciplined Habits*

*"If you want to change the world, start off by making your bed."*

— WILLIAM H. MCRAVEN

These words above in quotations were spoken by Navy Admiral William H. McRaven at the commencement ceremony at the University of Texas in 2014 where he addressed a huge student body. "If you can't do the little things right, you will never do the big things right," he said to the students. He went on to explain that life is a lot about getting the little everyday details right.

Besides pointing out the benefits of making one's bed every day (how during days that have gone tough or challenging, a well-made bed will prove to be a friend and source of comfort in the night) and recommending carrying the habit consistently throughout one's life, Admiral McRaven also points to the habit as a symbol of dedication to the little things that can prove to be a strong support to us in our lives.

There is an important lesson here for those wanting to become leaders: For one who can take on the responsibility of a whole battalion, classroom, government, company, etc., their first job every day is to take responsibility for their own personal life and that includes everything on the practical plane of existence. It's important to take care of ourselves first.

***Techniques for Cultivating Discipline in Everyday Life***

Taking further inspiration from his words, we can apply his teaching of *"taking care of the little things"* in a variety of ways. Here are some unique and creative ways in which we can further strengthen our personal and professional lives using Admiral McRaven's words of inspiration:

- **Conveying the deepest of feelings**, or our goodwill to others, through the simplest of words, gestures, and actions, and making our own positive intentions consistent. This would mean trying to give up moodiness in our relationships.

- **Keeping one's office or workspace organized**, neat, and clean at all times, we can again find a simple habit such as this beneficial and reliable for us for every stage in our professional careers.

- **Being disciplined about any physical exercise goals** we set for ourselves, even if it's only once a day. Make sure to do it, and be regular.

- **Being accountable for every promise we make to someone in our life.** If you say to someone you're going to do something, go ahead and make sure you do it. An accruing benefit from this will be that in a relatively short duration, people will come to respect you for keeping your word. Your clients will be more likely to become returning clients.

- **Encouraging growth in our circle of friends, family, colleagues, and the world** by offering to them whatever will prove as a guide/right advice (when it seems appropriate). As a leader, whether taken metaphorically, or literally, you may find that you are not able to enjoy the company of others owing to the fact that you may sense others' actions aren't going in the right direction. At such times, silently nudging someone in the right direction is a far better choice than to enter their confusion or misguided idea of enjoyment.

# BUILDING A CULTURE OF ACCOUNTABILITY

*Strategies for Fostering Accountability*

## Loved Ones and Accountability

When you are aware that others in your company are consistently making certain kinds of choices, despite the suggestions offered by those with higher wisdom, it is best to let them be accountable for those choices. Offer them the freedom to follow those choices and see where they lead. This feat, especially if those you are close to are concerned, requires exceptional non-attachment and letting go.

## Accountability in an Organization

When it comes to training in an organization, such as the armed forces, one's accountability is more toward others like superiors and whatever mission every member is faced with for the sake of their country or state.

During such instances, when you and others are united by a common overarching goal and are collaborators in the achievement of that goal—it's important to outline expectations. If someone's work is under your supervision, and they are answerable to you as an authority, letting them know your expectations and making them aware of the quality you expect is of paramount importance, even if you sympathize with them or their condition. Building an idea or approximation of something that an individual can deliver, is a wise thing to do. But at the same time, be open to building awareness and intuition about their actual realities and what may be holding them back from an excellent or ideal performance. Being sensitive to their needs or realities is still important.

Knowing the difference between an egotistical element holding someone back and an actual exigency or genuine need holding them back is important here. Interestingly, this applies to students as well.

**Students and Accountability**

When it is a question of students in your care or those you must train for the sake of their own education, it's important to instill in them the quality of being accountable to their own "higher self," or noble self, and being answerable to a developing conscience. Students can also be made aware that it is their duty to answer to anyone whose realities they may be stepping on. Discipline that teaches sensitivity to others' realities is the right approach for children, teens, and youth. It is important to motivate students enough to get them to the point where they are willing to see another's reality, and be accountable to themselves and to others through the right behavior.

**When Laying Out Rules and Guidelines for Teaching Accountability to Students**

In the case of teenagers or children, it is important to understand that teens are getting to that stage when they need to understand two things: what they owe to themselves as a duty (to one's personal growth), and what they owe to a group (dorm, classroom, home, community, school) as a positive contribution/duty. In one sense, both duties will help them grow at a personal level. But for accountability sake, they must learn to do both, not just one or the other.

Younger children will need a similar understanding of duties, though they will also need more acceptance from those in teaching positions (should they mix up the two duties, and confuse one for the other) due to the fact that young children ordinarily need to be rewarded for any positive efforts they make towards being better behaved, or performing well. These come under "duties to themselves" but we must allow for thinking of them as "contributions" as well. Good demeanor/lack of rowdiness, for example, (a duty to themselves) makes a drastic difference to the rest of the class/group/school as well and can be considered a positive contribution too.

## Making Your Own Self Accountable to Yourself

The best way to be productive, and far-reaching in one's impact both personally and professionally, is to make it about what you put yourself through; what you hold your own self accountable for. For example, keeping your integrity for the sake of inner satisfaction. Doing the right thing, not for showing to someone else, but because it feels right in your own heart.

### *Case Study: Successful Team Transformation Through Accountability*

Chris Hadfield, an astronaut, engineer, and pilot who was named the Top Test Pilot by both the US Airforce and US Navy is named also in Canada's Aviation Hall of Fame. He's authored the book called *An Astronaut's Guide on Earth*, and was the commander of the International Space Station when he was in space for five months. He's also been the Operations Chief for the ISS at NASA, as well as NASA's

Director of Operations in Russia. From these diverse experiences in leadership, Colonel Hadfield has taught some very important tactics that worked for him as a leader and a manager of diverse teams with varying levels of complexity involved:

- Making sure your team members have a say in some of the decisions you make.
- Building a sense of trust and camaraderie between team members since every now and then mistakes may happen, and focusing on the good at such times is very important.
- Respecting culturing differences, and celebrating diversity as that enables using all the expertise available. Even similarities in upbringing can sometimes teach different approaches through culturally different team members.
- Keeping calm and having a balanced perspective in extremely tough situations. Keeping in mind that such things as pandemics, wars, etc. have been faced by mankind before as well.
- Celebrating little victories, and big accomplishments as well—both are equally important.

## EMPOWERING OTHERS THROUGH ACCOUNTABILITY

### *Balancing Discipline and Empowerment*

- **The restrictive vs. the expansive:** If one thinks of discipline as a restrictive energy, and empowerment as a more expansive, freeing energy, then yes, the two need to be balanced well. But if you consider freedom and empowerment to stem from discipline, then they are one and the same thing.
- **Discipline empowers:** It's often shown in martial arts that the more disciplined and effective someone is in their techniques, the more power there is. The more control we have over our minds, the more power results.
- **When disciplining someone other than yourself:** Employ the use of discipline with compassion. Never resort to harshness that can kill someone's cheerful spirit. Discipline that is too harsh has dire consequences—it can harden people, deaden their sensitivity towards others' realities, or take away their hope, sense of self-respect, or the will to survive. Too much discipline in one go breaks the spirit. Discipline needs to be balanced and appropriate. Keep in mind others' realities even if pushing their limits.
- **From disciplining to empowering through teaching:** The goal of life is to have fun—approach leadership with the same attitude. Try to see it as bringing people joy, security, happiness, camaraderie.

Don't view your position (of a leader/pioneer) as a burden, or leadership as a burdensome profession. If you view the unpleasant parts of leadership, things like being stern with others, disciplining, giving consequences, or helping them face mistakes, and blunders, allow these to become opportunities to teach wisdom, though not explicitly. You can start viewing it as helping others be open to changing, learning, and growing from their mistakes.

- **Empowerment through life skills:** Leadership of a true kind, in fact, comes with an obligation to teach a little bit about life itself- even if you are focusing on one discipline/ subject/department. How people do their work is very much related to how they live their lives and who they are—it's these that reflect and come across in their work. Hence, there is always room for approaching the question of "life skills." The military is a discipline among others, from where we can draw numerous life skills. Military leaders or those who learned how to be leaders after being in the military often share important life lessons.

### Stories of Leaders Who Empowered Their Teams Through Discipline

Here are two famous examples of empowering teams through discipline both from ancient times:

- There is a story demonstrating the power of discipline on the mind. The story dates back to ancient India, where a young warrior prince by the name Arjuna, and his brothers and cousins, were being trained in the art of archery by their Guru/teacher named Dronacharya. When it was Arjuna's turn to aim the arrow, he said the following words to his teacher, upon being asked what he was aiming at, "I see the head of the bird." The teacher asked additionally, "Anything else?" and the student replied, "Nothing else, only the eye of the bird." He then let the arrow loose, and it hit its mark. The concentration he'd developed was such that he obliterated all other images and distractions while taking the shot. No other student had this level of discipline, but they learned from his example.

- William of Normandy was a duke who never gave up. He set the same example for his entire army. He never gave up in the face of obstacles or failures. By being the bravest leader and warrior himself, he led his armies in that spirit and conquered England in 1066 at the Battle of Hastings. After that event, William became known as William the Conqueror, and was crowned as King of England, following which the English became known as one of the most disciplined countries in the world. England, though small in size compared to many countries, sent its armies and colonized many different nations around the world for several centuries since then. It was on the strength of their discipline that they could achieve such victories.

### *Goal-Setting and Accomplishment*

Goal setting is a good and helpful skill to have if we are to conquer a big task in front of us. Accomplishments and achievements happen when we've been able to bring into practice a good degree of discipline, effort, and accountable action toward our goals—both big ones and simple ones.

*"Discipline is the bridge between goals and accomplishment."*

— JIM ROHN

- When we approach a particular goal, dream, or desire, we sometimes find ourselves confused in a labyrinth of ifs and buts, and how's and why's, etc. Not having a clear way to get where we want to go in life can be a challenge. But if we break up our journey or process into tiny segments and "achievable goals," it can start to look a lot easier, and accomplishment then doesn't seem hard.
- With goal setting, and accomplishing numerous goals one by one, one step at a time, we can develop the confidence in ourselves to keep going and feel happy with every effort.
- These tiny/mini-goals need to be very simple, and something you can see yourself accomplishing easily, preferably a day at a time, or even an hour at a time.
- Focus and discipline are key here. If you can discipline yourself in such a way that you simply refuse to allow yourself to get distracted by the daily interruptions of people's calls, emails, guests visiting, social media influence, or even worries about how to

pay bills, it will bring an ever deeper calmness and one-pointedness to the goal-fulfilling process and you will get there.

## PRACTICAL EXERCISE

- Listen to the following talk on discipline and accountability in your free time:

  - Account by Jocko Willink—Why Discipline Must Come From Within You:

- Reflection, self-study, being true to yourself, self-honesty, and introspection can help you understand how and in what way you can be accountable to yourself and your goals. Create a habit of journaling about your goals, and how you see yourself, with all the strengths or weaknesses you have, attaining your goals.

CONCLUSION

The next chapter will discuss decision-making under pressure and possible scenarios leading to decision-making, as well as scenarios caused by decisions gone awry. The preparation involved and the needed initiatives will be discussed, as well as how to handle the most important decisions on a day-to-day basis (the crucial backbone structure that supports all your other decisions related to work and personal life).

# DECISION-MAKING UNDER PRESSURE

*"Am I being helpful here, or hurtful?"*

— SAYING FROM LIVING WISDOM SCHOOLS

## CONSIDERING EXTREMES DURING DECISION-MAKING

Navy Seals Jocko Willink and Leif Babin share in several of their talks the importance of considering the dichotomies of leadership and these are especially important to consider during decision-making situations. Other noted authorities in leadership have also commented on the importance of knowing wise decision-making in the thick of pressure. The following are some key takeaways from different sources.

### The Importance of Patience in the Face of Mistakes

It is very important to have the patience to see others make mistakes (this is one reason why it's important to understand whether you are helping someone grow, or making a drastic decision like firing someone). For, if your subordinates or mates feel under pressure all the time to be perfect, it may break their spirit eventually and also hinder the possibility of them developing into their full potential. Everyone becomes perfect by trying to be better and better. It's a process, and repeated mistakes are the components of this process. Always accepting that there's a "better" way to perform needs to come with every step.

Admiral McRaven calls it "Getting over being a sugar cookie, and keeping on moving forward." The important point to get here is that one simply is a "sugar cookie"—meaning imperfect. And this is why the goal is always "improving" one's performance with time.

It is important, however, to understand when is an extreme action called for, and when one should avoid an extreme.

### Seeing Others in Terms of Their Potential

Try to see others in terms of their potential, instead of that which they are lacking. While it is good to keep track of things your team members or subordinates need to strengthen, it is also very crucial for the success of an endeavor to trust your team and believe in their capability to become excellent. A good leader must be willing to see a soldier in terms of his most recent transformation, and not always in terms of what any past record may show about him. Tuning into the past too much can hinder our trust and faith in another's potential and make us blind to recognizing their growing capability. Be in the present.

This principle applies to family, old and new friends, partners, and others as well.

### *A Call That is Meant for You to Take*

Decision-making can sometimes come in high-pressure situations; crucial moments when no one is there to help you. You may also find that others, even if they are in a position to help you, may not understand the full ramifications, possible repercussions, and possible consequences of the decisions you make. In those situations, you are obliged to trust your own knowledge and intuition. These can apply to time-sensitive situations as well, because it is possible to make decisions in very little time even against impossible-seeming odds.

## BEING PREPARED FOR THE WORST

Decision-making done under pressure of any kind can go wrong. In other words, yes, mistakes do happen! In such cases, whether due to others' bad decisions or ours, we need to be prepared for the outcomes. Worst-case scenarios are not just a result of decision-making gone wrong, they are also times when one's decision-making abilities get tested.

*Hypothesize the Worst Consequences, and Be Prepared In Case They Happen*

Consider the following:

- **When you need to hypothesize and plan accordingly:** When COVID hit the world, a lot of planning began to happen to understand how to deal with it, and get going on the execution of that plan. That is one example of hypothesizing as the problem was unfolding in a hidden way. A lot was unknown, and planning involved anticipating the impact it was going to make as it spread. Measures for mitigating the damage were put in place everywhere.
- **When a hypothesis turns into reality:** When one has very little time to respond and adapt, just go with the flow. There is a part of us that kicks in instinctively when things start to happen too fast— be it anything. Just remember, don't have the attitude of "not trying." The important thing is to "try" to deal with it, no matter how little control you have over the matter. For example, when physically disabled, try to affirm strength mentally. And vice versa if mentally affected. Running and physical exercise is a good affirmation of health when you're undergoing a mental health challenge.
- **When worst-case scenarios are experienced for the first time:** If you were not prepared, see these scenarios as learning experiences and just accept them for whatever they teach you. Do what you think is the sensible and appropriate thing to do rather than react, run away, or give in to any

weakness in mind or emotion. It's okay to vent for a while, but then buck up to deal with the situation.

- **The period after you faced the worst-case scenario:** You will come out with great appreciation for the simple joys of life, for every kindness, for everything that is tender and beautiful, and for everything noble, which is a cause for great inner happiness. You will also be much stronger than you ever were before.

### *The Secret to Endurance and Perseverance—Your Backup Plan Under Any Scenario*

- **The power of complete acceptance:** Acceptance of things as they are, in a complete manner, is what allows you then to shape them into what you would like them to be.
- **The power of pain endurance:** Be a buffer and accept the shocks that are coming your way. The ability to do this will take you on to the next level of maturity, wisdom, and heights as a human being and as a leader.
- **The show must go on:** No matter if the world is crashing, or thunder strikes, to name a few deadly scenarios, or equally heart-wrenching ones like betrayals or attacks from others, keep your head held high and remember that life must never come to a halt or be considered "not worthy" to move forward with. Things always solve themselves out, given time and patience. This is why the show must go on, because the show of this world has a deep meaning.

- **After complete acceptance, carve a new path and proceed:** Consider what you would like to do going forward, for a new path. It will involve letting go and learning to simply forget the old ways, people, situations, tracks, etc. because getting over setbacks takes time. Even if you return to something of the past, give yourself plenty of time to heal and recuperate, during which you create a safe and new life. "Walk like a Man," says a famous song, by J. Donald Walters, "even though you walk alone." Were your life to go back to something of the past, you'll still need a new way of approaching it. So focus on the "new."

- **Never think it's over, keep on moving:** Strange things also happen to us in life sometimes; unexpected things, among other challenges. The point is to never stop moving and never stop putting out efforts. Life basically is a battlefield. Things not in our control, or connected to us in a personal way, also happen. Circumstances just simply are unpredictable. But one's goals, and faith in a victorious life, and the hope of events unfolding in one's favor should not be given up ultimately. One must pick up one's sword, so to speak, and continue fighting the battle of life. One must continue to nurture dreams and hopes anew even when all seems lost. Every soldier coming back alive from a battle lost knows that the sacrifices made were not for nothing, and that life goes on—and battles continue for a good reason.

*Knowing All Steps of A Process Execution*

- **Know everyone's reality:** A leader or team manager must know all the steps involved in processes that must be undertaken by those who are working under them, and those employed by those who are under them—basically all the way down the ladder of hierarchy, a leader (and really anyone, not just those appointed as leaders) must be aware of the work involved, not for the sake of decision making or central control over every tier, but rather, for the sake of knowing the realities of everyone working in their system.

- **Be ready for action:** Accordingly, the leader must be able to be sensitive to those realities especially when hiring, training, paying, or offboarding are involved. More importantly, just as an army general would do this, a leader must know how to get down with the lowermost ranks of soldiers and fight hands-on when the need of the hour is to do just that—when it is called for, when no one else is there to do it, and the success of the mission depends on it.

- **It is your place to serve:** A leader must be prepared to do the most basic of the jobs within his or her organization if an important occasion comes up and the staff is experiencing shortage. Never think that because you are a leader, advisor, or leader figure, it is beneath you to get your hands dirty. Service is always the hallmark of a great leader.

- **Do your best, and leave the rest to fate/destiny/God:** Make sure that you are putting in your very best effort, and then allow yourself to feel free about the outcome. Attachment to what the outcome may be will not serve you well.

## MAINTAINING CALM

Maintaining calm is important for any kind of decision-making you do under pressure, or without pressure. A calm heart and mind ensure, in most cases, that your decision is going to be correct. At times, however, when one is already in a difficult situation, the choice is between which course will mean less suffering/damage, if not totally ensuring an escape from it. At such times also, one can employ calmness.

The important thing to understand is that calmness does not mean inactivity or paralysis.

Calmness gives you the ability to see a challenging or complex situation with a lot of clarity, which a restless mind will not allow you. When you are centered in yourself, in your calm self, in your spine (like soldiers and military personnel are), you develop the ability to go through any difficult situation with heroic courage.

*Every Challenge Needs You To Be Calm Or You'll Be Swept Away By The Tides of Trouble*

## Practical Ways of Being Calm In the Midst of Any Storm

- **Always being prepared for what life may bring** by keeping a regular meditation practice (daily if possible) that helps you calm the mind and heart.
- **Practicing peace, harmony, and acceptance** in all daily interactions with others (letting go of restlessness causing hobbies, or anything that disturbs the mind or aggravates the hormones in the body).
- **Choosing your challenges** in the sense that you can always be conscious of the number of choices you have in any given situation. When one kind of challenge seems hard to face, go after another challenge, face and overcome it; then come back to the previous one and make an attempt again.
- **Being okay with not having a choice sometimes:** Learn to be okay with having only one path facing you sometimes in a situation. Courage is required if it's a difficult task that life demands, and one where you know you should do it.
- **Developing perspective** is very helpful. Sometimes it seems that we confuse long-range happiness with short-term goals and vice versa. In such situations and other situations also require one to develop perspective, and the ability to compare things, people, and circumstances, in a non-judgmental way. This helps in further understanding "fair play" and what's "right/justified."

- **Most importantly, letting go of "self-preoccupation"** which is a big factor in moods, or feeling blocks in yourself—this factor can cause us to lose calmness and become emotional about our life. Think more about what you can do, rather than about who you are or what your image is.

### The Most Important Decision You Can Make Day-to-Day

- **The reality of who you are now and the hope of who you want to be:** You can decide at any given moment in your day how you want to "be." You could be touring some exotic location or you could be visiting family, having an ordinary day at work, or a day at home on the weekend—whatever the kind of day, or the kind of pressure or challenge you encounter, the most important thing to have at any time is the simple ability to choose how you feel. How you feel is a subtle mix and balance between reality and affirmation.
- **Raise your energy:** When you sense something is good, you naturally feel fine. Other times, you may be bored or lethargic. If it's these, you need affirmations that invoke your enthusiasm and motivation; in other words, you always need to "raise your energy" when anything downward pulling, heavy, or troubling happens.
- **Think in terms of how possible solutions/decisions will feel:** When something iffy, strange, confusing, or bad happens, or even something that needs urgent work under a time constraint, you need to think

about what is best (what is the solution) and for that, you need to know what the solution or the way out would "feel" like. You can bring to mind the vibe you want in response, or how you or people will adopt that solution you are thinking of, or react to it; how it would logically play out. But more than that, how the solution affects the feelings of those concerned. Without anticipating feelings, you wouldn't be able to hypothesize possible solutions very well.

- **Timing of decisions:** Sometimes a matter needs sleeping over, meditating on, or deliberating over. Other times, it doesn't need all that and, even against all odds, you can make an impossibly quick and spontaneous decision, maybe to the bafflement of others, but it turns out to be exactly what was needed. One should be prepared for either case.
- **Too much familiarity develops contempt:** The more one acts on grounds of familiarity, the sooner they will develop contempt for others. Try to strive for the "ever-new" where you normally don't look for it, and try the tried-and-tested way where you know it's appropriate and effective.

## PRACTICAL EXERCISE

- Got bad news? Energy hitting rock bottom? How do you want to feel the rest of the day? Can you put words to it? Can you choose an action or hand gesture to raise your energy and feel better despite the unfortunate news? These also help one to do something about it—cope with it, work with it, or turn it around.

- Affirming a sense of wellness, energy, and power will allow you to make good decisions. Make creative affirmations for yourself to rely on. For example:

  - "I am supremely content in myself."
  - "I feel great; I am free."
  - "Wisdom is my guide."
  - "Be patient and accommodating, but achieve your purpose." (This one is a reminder to be patient with a variety of people).
  - "I am happy and productive; my dreams are being fulfilled."

Repeat these affirmations under your breath, out loud, mentally, or in a whisper.

- Watch the following talk by a speaker breaking down Statesman General Collin Powell's 40-70 rule on good decision-making:

## CONCLUSION

In the next chapter, we will study leadership and hierarchy, and how the concept of hierarchy is applicable to your personal and professional life. There have been many monarchs, but few really know what the secret to excellent governance is. Let us study some of these secrets in today's modern world systems as they may pertain to you.

# THE IMPORTANCE OF HIERARCHY IN LEADERSHIP PRACTICE

*"There are leaders and there are those who lead. Leaders hold a position of power or influence. Those who lead inspire us. Whether individuals or organizations, we follow those who lead not because we have to, but because we want to."*

— SIMON SINEK

## LEADING OTHERS MEANS LEADING YOURSELF FIRST

### Be The Monarch of Your Life

- **Be happy, and be happy for happiness's sake:** Ask yourself, am I generally happy? How do I prioritize feeling happy—being truly happy, within?
- **Be in control of yourself:** Develop a meditation practice for calmness and self-control, even if it is 5-10 minutes in the morning, such that you learn to

control your subtle impulses and instincts and gain mastery over your energy, willpower, ability to think clearly, and to feel sensitively. In the same vein, try not to overindulge in sense pleasures like alcohol, sex, or television for the same reasons; they deaden the clarity in your awareness.

- **Don't always be led by habits:** Use your willpower consciously, and exercise the power of making choices. Habits can do good, but don't make habits the only performance indicators in your life. Sometimes, you may find yourself feeling bound by a thought, or feeling, a tendency, or a habit. In those cases, it is absolutely right to change the habit if it is crippling you, or break it and create flexibility in its place. For example, instead of feeling bound by an excess coffee drinking habit in general, or thinking that reading positive things or taking a mini-silence break are only things for the morning, try to break free from these habits or fixed thoughts and patterns. Don't beat yourself if you fail. Keep trying until you succeed. Be creative in coming up with solutions.
- **Seeking direction vs. seeking inspiration in one's life:** Many times, you need inspiration and that's perfectly good. Other times, it's more serious—you are looking for a real direction in life. Choose the right person or teachings to turn you in the right direction. Follow your heart. And once you've found the direction that is right, don't take counsel from others to "try new things" or "change that direction," for you can't walk in life with your feet in two different boats at the same time. Direction must come only from one source; inspiration can come

from anywhere. The two should not be confused with each other.

- **Taking care of oneself—healing on all levels, nurturing body and mind (inside and out):** Sometimes separation from others for a time is important so you can realize what you want to see happen in your life. One major realization had by people in such times is that their focus needs to be on nurturing themselves. It's another way of taking responsibility for one's own self—in fact, it's the foundation on which you build other things in your life. Always give priority to healing yourself on all levels, nurturing and nourishing through care and healthy habits. And practice supporting others as well in their journeys to heal and nourish themselves.

- **When you counsel others:** be ready to do those things yourself if needed, or have a regular practice doing those things which you are counseling others to adopt in their daily life. Also, try not to force any counsel on others, especially when they don't ask for it. Forcing them to adopt opinions, or pressurizing them in the name of counseling them, has many adverse and unwanted effects on others which will come back to you in time.

*Great Military Leaders Have A Common Message—Be a Source of Happiness/Inspiration for Others*

- **Why is being a source of happiness for others important?** Why is this trait important in a leader? Or in practicing leadership skills? We have many cases in history where leadership proved dictatorial and hatred-inducing. Hitler and Stalin are examples. Many a terrorist organization leader also comes to mind, don't they? We don't want to be the kind of leader who drives people in the wrong way. In fact, leadership isn't about driving people at all. Leadership that can inspire the masses, or people of a particular community (racial, religious, professional, or any other) to positive actions, and the actions that are kind and humanitarian in essence, and service-oriented to human beings and the planet, are the kind you would be remembered and cherished for.

- **The secret to progress (in a life led by the pursuit of happiness):** Learning to forget yourself in doing different activities. Always be busy with something or the other. This doesn't just have to mean "serving others" or "working in an office". It can also be forgetting yourself in playing a sport, creating a painting, cooking something at home, playing with children, or getting something nice achieved through the use of your hands, feet, body, mind, or voice, etc. Basically, anything productive that makes you forget yourself while your energy finds a useful way to channel itself. Once you get into the habit of always staying busy in this way, you will develop a high level of creativity, and the ability to stay happy, and can also develop the gifts of spontaneity and genius. This is an essential way a person can be the monarch of their life—always be engrossed in fun activities enough to forget yourself.

- **Stress vs. relaxation—meeting the challenges:** Make sure you experience a sense of relaxation through the activities in your life, even though actively engrossed in them. Deep fulfillment follows if you do this. Hard work, in other words, shouldn't feel like stress. Stress can eventually make you susceptible to being hurt by others (especially if you take on too many responsibilities) or to negativity in case disappointments come in your personal life. Hence, always find part of the day to do something that deeply relaxes you. It will ensure you are for the most part positive. And in doing this, others will always find you to be a source of happiness, even if you don't do anything out of the way for them. Your mere presence will be a comfort to them because they will feel your own calmness and serenity due to higher chances of your being positive.

- **The importance of solitary walks:** You can sort out a lot of stuff going on in your life if you actually take walks alone. Walking with others, be it family or friends, makes it a social call, whereas walking alone makes it an important appointment with your higher self—that part of you that wants to tread the best, highest, and wisest course in life. There are amazing things you can realize about your life, and about yourself, if you walk alone and also mentally share thoughts with yourself and address them to God (if you're a person of faith). Have a way of opening your heart and sharing your thoughts with someone or something up there who knows us to our very core.

- Many great leaders lived by the teachings of this saying: "**Seclusion is the price of greatness.**" Being alone for long periods develops you in ways you normally would never be able to develop if you continued to be with society and the crowds all the time. Great leaders often retreated to places of solitary seclusion to find the answers to difficult situations in their lives, and others' lives. Once they came out (some did this for years), they had amazing wisdom and a spirit rich with treasures (practical, scientific, revolutionary, etc.) that proved helpful for all humanity. For example, George Washington Carver, Joan of Arc, and many others.

### *Establishing Independence In Your Career and Profession*

### Consider Establishing A Unique Way to Make Money

If you find yourself running into unemployment for reasons not under your control, try setting up something independent of companies and employers. Become your own boss.

### Start Your Independent Venture With a Blueprint

Make a blueprint/map/flow chart/outline/visual of your goals, dreams, and ideas, so that they can be easily visualized and brought into existence. It helps to ideate something before you start actually creating it. Leaders like captains of ships all have a map to work with. Teachers have lesson plans. An architect creates a blueprint of the layout of the building before beginning work. A designer makes a drawing first, a writer makes an outline, a software engineer makes flow charts, and the list goes on. A healer imagines/visualizes the healing in the form of colors and animations to affect the actual healing in the body. Most intellectual work needs a blueprint. Brainstorming and recording it in the form of notes also works.

## You'll Want to Earn More Over Time, So Study How You Can Expand Your Services

See how you can expand your reach/services every decade of your life. This will ensure you can have stability in life, and something to call your own as life progresses. A home, a car, an emergency savings fund, etc. are all things you could look into having over time, if not in your twenties or thirties.

## How Much Do You Like Your Job or Should You Seize An Opportunity Coming Your Way?

Oftentimes, the victory is in being able to anticipate a challenging opportunity as a fun adventure, rather than seeing it as a daunting task that you feel like giving up on because you feel too dry to appreciate it, or consider it unworthy. In other words, oftentimes things/opportunities are worth considering and pursuing; after that, whether you sign a contract or not, is a different matter. Due consideration (for a possible direction) can be a key component in hitting upon unexpected prosperity and success.

If you don't like your work or job, consider bringing fresh attitudes, and the best and most honorable qualities to your work environment. Give it the very best you've got—then see what comes of it. Does life release you from that job role? Or promote you? Or show you another job that you'll actually find more meaningful? One of the three is bound to happen when you create a sustained period of excellent energy outpour.

## HIERARCHICAL RELATIONS IN ORGANIZATIONS

*Undercurrents*

- **Being aware of financial undercurrents in an organization:** A major concern most people go through is the "allocation of resources." In companies, where stakeholders are present, ones with an active board of directors, investors, etc. every position held by someone comes with certain promises and obligations which may not be known to people other than the directors. A smart leader would know how to sense the subtle undercurrents of resource allocations, position assigning, and company goals allotted to each position.
- **Overcoming competitiveness:** By sensing the undercurrents in hierarchy, you can learn to put aside frustrations related to not being recognized and rewarded for any exceptional work you did. Competition and jealousy come in when someone doesn't see you as a contributor. You can aid in overcoming competitiveness by taking the help of those you know are loyal to righteous conduct in your organization.
- **Passing the baton:** Have a strong foundation on which to build a legacy you can pass on someday, even if you are not the leader to begin with.

Whatever you do, your service must be transferable as no duty or service really stays with time. Everything changes and transitions with time. Try to see your duty as something in your keeping till the next person comes on board. When they come, pass it to them graciously, even if you are being fired. Be absolutely firm in your foundations, so that the next person will be able to pick it up easily.

*Relationships*

- **Treat every expert/pro opinion of accomplished individuals with an even-mindedness.** In this way, you will always speak to "higher position" people with a down-to-earth quality, and that will only go to show that you treat them the same way you treat yourself and others—as humans; as equals. Putting anyone on a pedestal has to be done carefully and only in cases where you know someone is truly deserving of honor. It's also safer to treat someone with exceptional regard and respect if you first find them to be humble. Otherwise, your feelings could get hurt if someone, out of ego, disregards you despite your sincere adoration/admiration for them. Try never to flatter anyone just because they're in a high position—that will only bring a very disappointing experience of "coming down to Earth" in due course of time.
- **If you are a leader, try to recognize and reward the creative and helpful ideas** of employees of every tier in your organization. It shouldn't matter whether it's an office clerk or a higher-level administrative

member. Also, simply because you are the leader, it shouldn't stop you from having a relationship with any member of your organization. True leaders ask others in their team about their welfare, feel concern when some tragedy strikes, and help out when they find themselves in a situation where others need an extra hand. A true leader is considerate and helpful toward everyone in the team/company/unit/battalion etc.

- **Sometimes your efforts to be kind to your subordinates**, and establish a relationship with them, will be wasted and nullified due to a second authority nullifying the effects of your power/position/duty. It shows a lack of a desire to collaborate on their part, and it could be a bad leadership case if the second authority is on a higher wrung than yours and bent on achieving their own goals.

## EFFECTIVE PERSONAL AND PROFESSIONAL GROWTH IN A HIERARCHICAL ENVIRONMENT

*Practice Initiative—It Stands Out in Hierarchical Environments as Having its Own Power*

- **Become a cause, not an effect—don't wait for success to knock at your door, go and meet it halfway:** Leadership, the ideal, requires consciously cultivating attitudes of leadership as you go along in life; it takes initiative. More and more, when you become the reason for there to be joy, empathy, understanding, efficiency, energy outpour, and organized functioning in your own life, you start affecting everyone around you in a positive way. Then no more are you waiting for circumstances to bring you happiness—you take the lead in creating such momentums. You take the initiative to get good processes started, even if they are for yourself alone.

- **When you're magnetic, others want you:** Pretty soon, you find that you are in demand, and companies want to hire talent like yours as managers, mentors, directors, or even the face of their brand—simply because you create opportunities and positive workflows where there were none to begin with. You are an active cause and agent in productivity, success, and positivity coming about for an enterprise. It may be a personal life habit, but that ability you develop will exert itself in every sector of your life. You'll develop the ability to attract success, and others will want you for you will become an asset. It is a principle of life.

- **One doesn't always know everything, and that's okay!** Facts, for instance, or vocabulary, or the latest news, etc. It's alright. It's okay to not know and be frank with others that you don't know something. Part of being human is accepting the limitations of being a human. A vast vocabulary or a roster of facts must not be confused with wisdom. Those who are truly happy, and who enjoy their life, don't need to know much about this world, even while employed in a profession and out in society. Accept that you don't owe it to others, or to society, to know everything.

### *Questions to Ask Yourself for Professional Growth in Hierarchies*

**Goal:** Exploring the needs of your people/team/audience/customers in an all-rounded way. That means thinking out of the box as well, something that goes the extra mile to help out the others whom you are serving, even in unusual ways sometimes.

For example, you could ask yourself the following questions:

- How do I feel working with this person?
- What do I want to give them?
- How do they feel about my work?
- Am I, and my service, the right choice for what they need or want?
- Is my skill set up to the mark for meeting their needs?

Allow yourself to work with the thought of gratitude for the ones you are serving. Always focus on the thought of "giving" to them. You are, after all, entrusted with their care and well-being through the services you give them, and how you handle their affairs.

## CONCLUSION

To conclude, be the sole monarch of your life. You may want to keep in mind to not feel bound by any hierarchical structures in the sense that you can still grow and create your own success in a company/organization/group. It's ultimately who you are as a person, and with what level of accountability you bravely and boldly aim to serve others out there which will make an impression on everyone. While it may seem like monarchs or heads of institutions have all the growth and success, one who dares to be bold in their service will have his own well-earned success without necessarily the high position. In the next chapter, we will explore collaborations.

# SETTING THE EGO ASIDE FOR A POSITIVE COLLABORATION

*"If I have the belief that I can do it, I shall surely acquire the capacity to do it even if I may not have it at the beginning."*

— M. K. GANDHI

## IF YOU WANT TO CHANGE OTHERS, CHANGE YOURSELF

### Every Challenge is About Making War On A Part of Our Own Self

Contrary to what war, challenges, or complex human relation scenarios may seem like, which is fighting against another—another's opinion, another's cause, or actions, the actual war for all of us is against that same quality or tendency within ourselves. Anything we strongly dislike, we also dislike in our own self. This is why, when we see that quality in others, we want to "oppose it" because we don't agree with that quality or energy.

Out in life, in a world not literally at war, the battlefield still exists. We're always up against parts of our own self (what part of us supports the higher choices, what part supports lower roads, what parts are strong, and which ones are weak or susceptible, etc.).

And of course, there's also a constant battle of choices we fight out in the world regarding those others than ourselves —like in our choices of a president, or supporting one charity as opposed to another, or finding one school better than another, or one brand more effective than another, etc. Again, it's a process of supporting one intention vs another or one quality vs. another.

For some, the choices they make in life are as stark as "fighting the darkness," metaphorically speaking. However, in fighting the darkness, or those things we are against that we do not believe in, that are ethically or morally wrong, we need to focus on the light—those positive things that are the opposites of the unwanted qualities. It's been said that the way to fight darkness is to turn on the light!

We may sense qualities in others that are not good; we may sense them in our own selves. We need to wage war on parts of ourselves that aren't right or good and those parts that don't support our highest interests in life. These are the qualities of a true leader.

### *Being Flexible is Part of Changing Ourselves*

- **Being tentative in some cases is helpful:** Part of leading yourself or others is knowing how to be flexible. When committing to a job or commitment/appointment with someone or a service you perform for them, part of what you promise should be kept in a tentative spirit, while other parts can be more definitive. It's a wise approach if you don't make rigid commitments that sound like broken promises if circumstances change and actually require us to reschedule, shift, or change an original plan/direction.

- **Choose fluidity Instead of rigidity:** Too much committed energy in one idea, method, or direction leads to bumps and falls (at a time of change) as opposed to a smooth direction/idea change when you have flexible energy; with a fluid approach, you can easily change the course of a project/activity, etc.

- **Create and recreate yourself** through the habits you have and take on. Think of it as chiseling yourself daily into a masterpiece. For example, read often— make time for reading and absorbing the things you read. Philosophers, famous scientists, scriptures, good wholesome literature—these will develop your intuitiveness about life, its experiences, and what's possible in our development as human beings. Choose any word or topic as your curiosity hook and google it. Becoming a netizen (an internet citizen) on the side is a very fruitful and rewarding thing to do alongside your profession, studies, or service. You can become an expert conversationalist as well, if that is something you desire.

- **Have a growth mindset:** Never give into the thought that certain goals and ambitions aren't achievable. Never admit defeat in that way, no matter the competition. If you have a dream—dare to manifest it and do it well. If it's hard to believe in a particular dream (because it's too good to be true, or too high an aim) *try* to believe it, even if it seems irrational. There is true power in the believing and aligning of one's actions with one's belief. This is also the advice of Sir Anthony Hopkins, an Oscar winner from Hollywood, considered a legend in the world of movies by many. Believing is a rare and important leadership quality—a practical one, though at first it seems impractical. Don't turn down phenomenal dreams by saying they are impractical.

- **Do it now:** It has been said "Now is the time for every good thing." Even if all you do is just start working on a goal, and go at a slow pace, that is far more important than never starting. Leaders take the initiative to keep nurturing their dreams, even if it's one step at a time, or even one year at a time. You can build success one step at a time. Gandhi said a very powerful statement once: "If I have the belief I can do it, I will surely acquire the capacity to do it, even if I may not have it at the beginning." You can develop the capacity over time to accomplish that dream or goal. All you need to do is start working on it in the present, and grow in that direction.

## POSITIVE COLLABORATIONS WORK ONLY IF THERE IS HARMONY

### *Harmony Happens Only When We Are Positive and Foster Positivity*

Things happen in every collaboration and every project. Things go wrong, and someone wants to lay the blame on someone or the other. It turns messy sometimes, and more often than not, people's sentiments are hurt. There are ways to bring harmony instead in tricky and challenging situations:

- **Blame not the person, Only their actions:** Based on critiquing someone's actions, a lot of constructive change and progress can be made. But blaming the character of a person is downgrading them because it leaves no room for recognizing the goodness that is within—the good parts of them, that which abides by the honorable things—or the change that they can make.

- **Focus on what's needed, not what was done:** If the person working under you has made blunders, even then, for leaders to do that which is best in a calm and impartial way is better (speak of the change needed) than to confront someone with their faults. Most people won't take it either. Only a few who are especially humble will stand such a trial and those are very hard to find. For another reason, it is better to focus on the positive change you want—that by blaming you may bring someone's morale down. It comes across as being harsh or insensitive to them in some way. Also, some are more sensitive by nature in matters of their faults. Speak of the thing that needs to change.

- **Approach life experiences like a leader with deeper insights:** Is something really what it seems to be, or what it says it is, or what it projects itself to be? This will enable you to anticipate failures before they even come or to see through people, or their work/creations, for what they really are. In doing the above, always go for the bird's eye approach instead of a haggler's approach. This means that rather than feeling cheated due to any insufficiencies, imperfections, or dishonesties in others, choose to have the bird's eye view—see the situation from above, keep your heart's feelings untouched and away, and take the course of action that will prove best for the other person (even if it means turning them down or not engaging further) and prove best for you. The bird sees everything from above, flies in freedom, and then swoops down only to one chosen desired place.

- **Respond appropriately:** You may be going through a lot inwardly at any given time, but always respond appropriately to others, keeping in mind their realities. Don't make a conversation about you. Don't be like a boss who enters the office and dishes out at others their mood, or with goals that are indifferent to what's going on in everyone else's life.

- **Avoid major and minor conflicts at work or home:**
  Avoid confrontations and jumping down the wrong
  hole by preferring mitigated and calm "facing the
  facts" with someone.

### *People Need to Be Heard in Good Faith*

- **Listen to others more:** Know how to listen when
  you are with others.
- **People are more important than things.** Give more
  preference to your team's growth than to the
  delivery of something absolutely perfect—it is more
  important that they learn from mistakes than the
  material world project being placed on the highest
  pedestal.
- **Try to have an understanding of others** even if you
  don't see things the way they do. Have the calmness
  to say the things which you want to say, while
  accepting others for what they say. Hear them out
  first, and then say what you must say. Statesman
  General Collin Powell also practices this method.
- **Know your team members well:** Understanding
  others in terms of who they are and what their
  dreams and aspirations are instead of who they
  follow on social media and what pictures they post.
- **Recognize the importance of giving your team
  something to put their faith in:** What would you
  have your team believe despite the reality of a
  work/mission/project? And what would you have
  them realize? Truth is the reality at a given time (the
  reality of aptitude, performance, and the

understanding of how a job is to be done, and when done, even the reality of having certain flaws showing up in one's performance, or a shortcoming that is evident) and truth that you would have people believe in, beneficial truths (statements like: "You can do much better," "I trust you will do everything to accomplish this," "Keep at it, and you'll be past the challenge soon," or "It's not what I expected, but it's something") form a delicate balance. The second is an important component; it's what you would have someone work towards or believe. Thoughts have power. Nurture those thoughts in them that will help them feel inner strength and fortitude.

## SEEING COLLABORATIONS AS DEVELOPING PEOPLE'S CHARACTER, CALIBER AND SKILLS

- **You can develop your team especially by modeling positivity** and fairness under all circumstances. Remember to cater to the needs of each one and in that way become true to your intention of being fair to all if you want them to learn to develop this quality.
- **Affirm the highest potential in yourself and others:** Letting go of self-definitions means affirming the best for yourself, in terms of what you may be capable of, and giving yourself time and chances to develop those capabilities. The same applies to others—give them opportunities and incentives to develop a higher performance or potential.

- **Work with everyone's strengths:** Encourage others' strong points in the carrying out of whatever project you do together.
- **Set an example for others and show them what strengths can achieve:** Leadership is about living for ideals and being an example for others in that spirit. Principles and ideals exist for a reason, and they are there for our happiness. Use those to show others and set an example of what can be achieved.

## PRACTICAL EXERCISE

- Watch this video on Statesman General Collin Powell's advice on leadership and teamwork. It is truly inspiring and uplifting.

## CONCLUSION

To conclude, always try in every collaboration to first see if you can change something about yourself, and it's a good practice to have throughout life. Harmony, above everything else, is the way to work and collaborate in a way that will be smooth for everyone involved. Finally, help your team members grow and evolve, even if it is uncomfortable for them sometimes. Leadership and collaboration is all about growing together as a team. In the next chapter, we will explore duties and responsibilities.

# ALLEGIANCE TO ONE'S DUTY

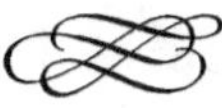

*"The greatest oak was once a little nut who held its ground."*

— ANONYMOUS

## TAKING RESPONSIBILITY

### Who Do You Have A Duty Toward? And What Are You Responsible For?

Who do you have a responsibility toward? As citizens and countrymen, military figures and leaders, soldiers, statesmen, and veterans, feel a sense of duty toward their country. Many know from childhood that this is what they've come to do in life— train in the military, fight for their country, and/or offer military training and hone the skills of others who've come to serve the country in this way.

What is it that you feel naturally responsible for? And who are the ones you feel a duty toward? Here are a few things to think about:

- **Understanding what your duty Is:** It's not necessarily that which you are good at, or great at. While deciding on a course of action and direction, see if it's right for you. A way to figure this out is to ask yourself—is it increasing my sense of ego or this sense of being separate from others? Or is this line of work or duty helping me forget the ego, the little self, and feel expansive? Self-honesty is needed here.
- **Your "own" duty:** What is right for someone else may be wrong for you, and vice versa. That's the reality. Everyone needs to follow their "own" duty. It is better to do your own duty, whether you fail or succeed, than to succeed in someone else's duty.
- **Professional life duties:** Agreed upon duties, smudging of the fine lines between your duty and someone else's duty (shared responsibilities), unclear terms in responsibilities and duties, avoiding too much burden, assuming "natural duties and responsibilities" at any time, avoiding "too little" responsibility—one's salary/payment must be commensurate with the amount of duty or responsibility, otherwise, consider it a warning sign (something may not be right if things are made too easy for you by an organization).
- **Personal life and duties toward one's family:** Try to see your duties toward your childhood family as equally important as your family from marriage. Respect, loyalty, harmony, and cooperation toward

supporting the family financially and emotionally are primary here.

- **One's duty in a bigger sense overall (in life):** The biggest duty of all, according to J. Donald Walters, is understanding that people are more important than things. Along with this goal, one must know that "where there is righteousness, there is victory." This is an ancient Sanskrit saying that is especially pertinent for leaders.

### *Mistakes Are a Part and Parcel of Being Human/Carrying Out Anything*

- **The important part is to always keep learning from mistakes:** They will come, they simply do! That's life! You can try and minimize them, but you can't eradicate them totally. Just like weather can't be controlled by humans, mistakes are like that too—many are unpredictable, and we learn only by going through them and looking back. By learning lessons from our mistakes, our future is always better than it would have been, even if not perfect.
- **Owning mistakes is important:** when it's yours, don't run away or be guilty. Never give in to guilt, even if you made a mistake. Accept that being a human, mistakes happen and that one is always learning to have better attitudes in life. In that way, owning a mistake is simply a normal part of life, not a cause for shame.

- **Some mistakes, problems, or battles lost don't affect the overall outcome—you still win!** In the overall war of life, of challenges, of dreams and goals, and of plans, to win the bigger war, if you end up losing a few battles along the way, it has been said (by J. Donald Walters, in his book *The Art of Supportive Leadership*), it's alright. In fact, it may be necessary to let go of a few wins, in order to succeed at the overall win/the bigger goal.

- **An example:** If you have been planning all along to impress your clients with a proposal, and have really worked hard on it, adding touches like presentations and visuals, don't freak out if a technical error happens last minute. Smart professionals don't need a lot of outer show. Who you are just comes across, and they know it when they see someone successful giving it their best shot with whatever they've got—a verbal speech, and body language—whatever it may be.

- **No effort is ever lost, despite mistakes:** Your client may still make a deal, or reschedule to give you an opportunity to present again. And even if they don't, all your efforts will not be in vain. Your next steps will unfold in a positive direction—it could be another way of utilizing that proposal you made. Hard work and effort are never lost, in other words. The energy put into something always makes a way to its match.

SERVICE

### *Position vs. Service and Humility*

- Being a leader, under any circumstance, means focusing less on the position or how glamorous it may be to be a leader or feel like one—it is more important to focus on the functions, duties, and work of the leader.
- Serving the organization/family/group/set of people/mission through the spirit you instill in others is the goal. That spirit needs to be of humble service.
- In one's family atmosphere, be "chivalrous" if you are in a courtship phase. This means that you must be courteous and gallant toward the other. It shows a service-oriented demeanor, and that says something; it's respectful. It is the quality of a true leader and anyone can do this.
- At other times, if it feels like you're having to bend over backward to serve another's needs, more likely than not, the other person needs to start doing a few things on their own. Leadership is serving another, but not spoiling them.
- In one's relationships in the personal life or the workplace: "Be Genteel"—The power of a conversation where you accept the outcome in good faith—and be prepared impartially whether someone is making a deal or not. That power will have a lasting impact, and that non-attachment to outcomes will always bring the best results. Lack of pushiness,

in other words, may be genteel, but also very respectful of others' realities. People appreciate this and do come back (which may seem unexpected) if they develop a good opinion of you.

In all of the above, we will notice that our manner of communication is important, but more than that, it is the attitude behind our words, and the feelings with which we imbue our words, that will come across to others as either helpful, simple, humble or smacking of ego.

LOYALTY

*How Loyalty Works in Professional Scenarios*

- **Be loyal to your life's experiences:** What they have revealed to you, and what they've shown you about others. In this way, when tough times come, you will still be loyal to those who have always been loyal to you.
- **Inspiration for work—love for work:** Choose devotion—do what you do for an ideal or for a muse, so to speak. Great works on the planet have been accomplished, works of art, literature, victories won by countries, and societies established because people had devotion to a cause, ideal, or someone they revered because of what they stood for, a quality they exemplified. It could be one's King or Queen for some people, it could be God or Christ for the religious-minded, or Krishna, Buddha, etc. It could be your mother or father that you dedicate your

efforts to. It could be someone you deeply love, who made sacrifices for you, that you devote your mind to when you work or perform your duties. Devotion is a beautiful and deep source of infallible strength.

### Be Loyal to Your Personal Growth and Progress

Here are a few ways you can be loyal to your personal growth and progress:

- Spend alone time regularly, reading books by great scientists, leaders, and philosophers. Think about the thoughts that were the reason behind great changes in civilization, people's contributions, and great systems and methods coming about. Write and journal about your reflections.
- Anytime you go through a video library, try to feel the consciousness behind the videos you browse through. Ask yourself which ones are helpful to you on all levels, and which aren't, even though they may seem to be popular.
- Try to see the correlation between your memory power and time spent on social media. Ask yourself if you feel more in command of your life with a greater memory power, or a shorter attention span which results from too much social media.
- When striking a deal with a client, try to understand whether it is actually going to be beneficial to you in ways other than just money. Take a decision based on everything that's going to be involved (on a personal level), rather than just the profit (which is a professional-level concern).

## CONCLUSION

Every human life comes with certain duties toward one's family, colleagues, and community. Being loyal to these duties and responsibilities is of paramount importance if we want to experience deep satisfaction and happiness. Service, humility, and an acceptance of the ongoing mistakes of life as part of carrying out our duties are the keys to understanding the deeper meaning behind leadership and the leadership approach. In the next chapter, we will be exploring diplomacy and resilience, which are necessary for tough situations in your personal and professional life.

# THE IMPORTANCE OF RESILIENCE AND DIPLOMACY FOR LEADERS

*"An easy life is not a victorious life."*

— PARAMHANSA YOGANANDA

One's leadership skills are especially tested when one finds themselves faced with extreme opposition—that's a time when you've got to take a tough call. Are you going to break under the immense weight and pressure, or are you going to endure? Resilience and diplomacy can help you endure.

## FINDING YOURSELF IN ENEMY TERRITORY

When finding yourself behind enemy lines, or when faced with outright betrayal in life, it feels similarly. It's basically when others persecute you.

The following are suggestions to keep in mind for being able to rely on certain approaches during tough times, you can strengthen some of the following in your life:

### *Being Inwardly Independent and Centered*

- **Always reserve the right to have your own understanding, and analysis** of the truth of an evolving situation (even if in front of others you are acting like you are going along with others' demands or thinking like they expect you to think)— something of a spy's job. Appearing dumb is helpful sometimes, and appearing smart in a completely different way than the actual reality, is also a smart move sometimes. These are methods of tricking your enemy. You may not know everything, but every moment unfolding reveals something. Understanding the deeper layers of a situation or person for that information can give you a way out of your difficulty sooner or later. It's like having a key out. Always keep an open and observant mind.
- **Render your enemy powerless** by being inwardly centered in your spine, no matter how acute the challenge, and by not accepting defeat mentally even if your body suffers. Withdraw your consciousness to your most inner self, where unbeatable calmness

and protection lie. Your inner self will always triumph—your power is inside. Nobody can take it from you. Try to maintain equanimity even in the face of extreme negativity, opposition, etc.

### *What You Can Do Without Letting the Other Know*

- **Being able to study and observe** your adversary's nature, behavior, motivations, and interests, while compelled to be around them, is a wise technique because the knowledge of things you notice about others may come in handy someday.

- **Being able to remain non-emotional in front of adversaries**, developing yourself in how you can simply let go of things in the moment in order to have the heart to face all circumstances, and resolve to persevere till you see the light of day again. When we become emotional, we may be venting, processing, or needing to cry, but it's also an affirmation of "sorrow" or a feeling of "all is lost"— never show these emotions to your adversaries. It may be true and natural that we simply need to express ourselves because after all we are human, but it's better to do it in private. It will help your efforts to win if you don't let them know what a struggle it is for you. It is part of showing someone that you've not accepted defeat.

*Calmness and Strength*

- **Remaining calm, or even pretending to be calm:**
  This can become your greatest weapon to pass
  through a mortifying, difficult situation, or actual
  enemy lines. You can choose to do this, even if
  difficult, when in the middle of an intense situation
  unexpectedly.
- **Relying on a technique that is a strength of yours,
  not just a technique that you happen to like:** There
  is a difference between a technique you can use in
  the spur of the moment and one you use only after
  having strengthened it and practiced it. Put
  differently, you may want to use a technique in an
  extremely rare situation, because you like its
  approach, and others are able to do it. But if it's not
  your strong suit, don't rely on it for chances are that
  it will fail you when a demanding situation comes
  up. Unless something is your strength, don't put the
  weight of a demanding situation on it.

## HANDLING STRONG OPPOSITION

The reason why opposition exists in our lives is to make us
strong in certain ways.

*Resilience in the Workplace*

**Understanding the world of affronts:** In one sense, no
affront in this world is personal. Most of the suffering we
may feel due to challenges in relationships and our profes-

sion can go away when we realize that nothing is in a sense personal. How? The following are some reasons:

- At any time in general, so to speak, what one is up against is what another person's current or past reality is—and that is to a large extent "things which pull on others' energies." Sometimes it means the choices and things others want to enjoy or give in to (even if negative). More importantly, it means commitments they have or the dreams they've been harboring, whether good for them or not good for them, are unknown to them.
- Nothing is in a sense personal, because others are usually going through something or the other. It could be the amount of pressure they experience, whether it's self-imposed or external, or it could be personal life sorrows that could have a bearing on their relationship with you and on their conversations with you.
- Sometimes, it's jealousy, but even that is not personal even if it seems that way. The reality of someone's jealous feelings could simply be a bad habit they have in general.
- Sometimes, others resent having done extra work because of any actions of yours, or your good intentions at refining a group project or needing a favor.
- When someone suffers due to something you weren't involved in, their attitude will reflect in their behavior, and if not in their behavior, then definitely in their aura, energy, and vibes (their magnetism).

Again, it's not as personal as it may seem. They've simply become that way.

**You can't change any circumstance professionally, or even personally, once it has happened**, but you can understand how to deal with it. Some things just aren't controlled by us. But we can train our minds, bodies, and habits, and learn to adjust and adapt ourselves; that has all the power to weather any storm, or any circumstance. It's not about what happens, it's about how you deal with it.

**Difficult scenarios with people:** Don't accept defeat mentally, even if outwardly you become a victim. Sometimes, we are beaten by something because we are under pressure of some sort, or some protection is lacking, or a need is not being met, among other factors. The actual problem or difficulty in many cases is solvable were we not under the strain. Hence, we can think of preparing ourselves well in case life gives us another such challenge again.

**Choose to remain untouched inwardly every time someone rejects you or doesn't believe in your positive potential:** This is especially true for those organizations that go through periods where a lot of firing of employees happens. If you happen to land in such a place and get fired for no fault of yours, choose not to take it personally. That which wasn't about you, need not be made about you, by you at least. You have the potential to have a lasting and enduring tenure with good organizations. You could also take it as a sign that you could start something of your own, independently. And don't carry any emotional baggage from any rejections.

**What to maintain always:** A phrase that can remind everyone practicing leadership tactics to be alert, vigilant, observant, analytical, and studious in their everyday work. Always have an agenda of studying every situation you come across, but in your relations with others, learn to come across as not having a personal agenda—it will help you accept the other's welfare (whatever that translates to in practical terms) as your goal at all times—and they will feel this sense of "no pressure" from you which will add a delightful energy to your interchange. If what you're offering as a service is wanted, take the offer calmly. If someone does not want what you're offering, accept it calmly, and look elsewhere for an opportunity.

*Resilience in Personal Matters*

- **Define challenges in your own terms:** You need to define the challenges in your own way and choose how you want to feel about them. In choosing, you can overcome every challenge. Just because others expect you to feel bogged down by the weight of their negativity, or someone else's negativity, don't feel pressured to think and feel along those lines—it would be giving into victim consciousness. Or if temporarily you fall into that, you can choose to bring yourself out of it and feel differently about the situation. Family members, especially those that are close to us, can give us inputs on how to see difficult personal matters, but always weigh the words of others inwardly and decide to feel positive and constructive, even if you haven't achieved your agenda of success in that situation yet.

- **Don't feel defeated just because others think of your challenges as defeats:** A lot of people don't understand that life is about falling and standing up, being beaten by tides of trouble, and yet not giving up; experiencing difficulty and yet succeeding in our goals, even if it takes years. Some might say that you're always having some challenge or the other. Others may say you haven't achieved anything of importance even though you've made so many efforts, etc., etc. Choose not to be bogged down by such comments. Respond to such people by telling them, for the sake of their own learning, that an easy life never was considered a victorious life on the stage of this world. In a way, the more troubles one experiences, the higher the chances of someone rising quite high in their personal attainments and professional journey, even if time is taken.

## COMMUNICATION

### *Speech and Its Implications*

### Diplomacy in Communication

There will come a point when giving onus to others, whatever good they are doing during whatever interactions you are having or outside of them—that attitude will become second nature.

Some may call this giving others the benefit of the doubt which, to be more precise, is giving someone the credit for being acceptable and speaking the truth, having good intentions, even if you are not sure that was the case.

**Encouraging Positivity, Even Tentatively, is Diplomatic**

Knowing how to deal with every kind of energy, opinion, suggestion, or thing said by someone, while also being impartial at the same time, ready for the least little sign of positive choice someone may show—a leader must know this. Be ready to offer encouragement when others make efforts in that direction.

**Say Only What is Necessary**

Speaking what is needed, but not reiterating yourself or the encouragement you offer; in other words, not overdoing the positivity. Sometimes situations afford the opportunity to speak more and offer extra encouragement to others, but it is better to use positivity and encouragement in tandem with someone's actual work and signs of progress in case they don't fulfill the minimum expectations in a work. This applies to communication with teenagers as well; encouragements need to be in sync with their actual performance, and teens need to know you're keeping track of their performance/developments or the lack of it.

**Speaking What is Needed, Not Just What is Expected**

This is again a leadership quality. Not just what you think superiors and others are expecting of you. It's never about looking prim and proper so that you appear perfect. Contrary to that, those who consider themselves pioneers or leaders (those having a place of service, in other words) must be able to remain flexible in their speech, showing an accommodating attitude by acknowledging contributions made by others, while at the same time offering their own unique insights on situations if they have them, both to their superiors, and those working with them, or under them.

## Verbalizing Things Vs. Non-Verbalizing

It is not always wise to communicate/verbalize/vocalize every time something objectionable happens in the universe, especially when it's one's personal and professional universe.

Analysis of others, or just hunches, or feelings/vibes you get from someone, about their understanding of life, situations, etc. should be kept in mind. What we observe is for us to decide what to do with it. Sometimes speaking to others is advisable; other times, it's not advisable to vocalize one's opinions or thoughts. We need to exercise discernment.

### *Speech and Emotions*

**Goal:** Being Able to Express Yourself Without Intense Emotional Overtones/Outbursts in Difficult Situations

- When you say something important (if you've been wronged, or are misjudged), without the emotional feel, whether it's written communication, spoken, or any other way, it will have a positive and effective effect. It takes effort to come to this point and requires working on oneself.
- Leaders, while they ideally should never support a lie being communicated in front of their eyes, should know how to refrain from getting angry when things

go out of hand because of "dishonesty" by someone. It is alright to object to a wrong thing, but not okay to treat it like an unimaginable crime.

- Often leaders are known to be angry or hot-headed. Deciding to be a leader who is especially positive, calm, and accepting in nature, but also efficient, requires wisdom and stamina.

- The ability to see both mistakes and successes and not react in extremes to either of these comes only with non-attachment to either.

- To have stamina is important as a leader. It refers to the ability to be a cushion in those circumstances when unexpectedly something bad happens or someone loses their cool or spoils an important matter. Maturity, patience, and stamina are the keywords here.

## CONCLUSION

Handling strong opposition or difficult scenarios and experiences can come as opportunities to learn resilience, the "never say die" attitude, and a way to practice calmness and inner strength. Diplomacy too comes in handy and is that delicate art that never fails to achieve its purpose if done with sincerity and goodwill. How we communicate is a big part of that. In the next chapter, we will discuss the relationship between freedom and power in leadership roles.

# FREEDOM AND WILL-POWER

*"It's not how many times you get knocked down that counts, it's how many times you get back up."*

— DAVID GOGGINS

## THE KNOWN RELATION (BETWEEN FREEDOM AND WILLPOWER)

With power in an organization or a group such as a government sector, comes the ability to make decisions that are not available to others—in this sense, this position comes with abilities. In fact, the effect of these decisions can influence every member of the organization/group. It can either be looked at as freedom—to be easy on others, or to be strict/harsh/manipulative etc., or you can view it as a binding of yourself to an ever-growing awareness of others and responsibility toward the organization and its members.

Many CEOs who are driven primarily by personal interest or monetary goals, and who sacrifice higher values in the process of administration, exercise insensitive use of power; equating it with freedom. If willing to learn the kind of leadership that is exemplary, freedom must only be exercised in the way of respecting others, understanding all realities, and going to great lengths to see that the right thing is done.

## THE NOT-SO-KNOWN RELATION

### *Willpower is of Two Kinds: Destructive and Constructive*

Power actually should not be looked at as freedom, for that which appears to be freedom is actually responsibility for constructive stewardship, ideally. To be a successful leader, it would benefit you to transform your willpower ability into constructive willpower exercised for the welfare of others.

Practical steps with insights from history and military leadership:

- **Claim the power within you:** But don't get carried away and hurt somebody with it. To be a leader, it is important to have a consciousness of power and it's essential to have that thought (you can sow it in your mind before sleep or after waking up) that you are powerful. Associate that thought with "life," "energy," and "the ability to dream, and do good in this world" regardless of how much competition there is. Your inner power is your throne. Claim it, and exude power, so long as you are not hurting anyone with it.

- **Work with the thought that there is a higher power working through you:** When you work with this thought, feel this power, which is the essence of all creation/manifestation in this universe of energy behind all matter. When you sense that this power has its own intelligence, conscious purpose, and skill, your performance will exceed your expectations and you won't even feel tired or exhausted after huge expenditures of personal energy. The thought of an infinite power working through you is actually powerful and affects performance and services in extraordinary ways.

- **The more centered you are in yourself, the more power you will feel; inner power Is lost when you hurt or dominate others:** In your personal or professional life, try not to assert your points or show power over another. You'll tend to do that when you feel that others have a hand in shaping your reality. Subconsciously, we may be handing the reigns of our feelings to others when we share them with them. If others don't respond approvingly, we may get frustrated due to a lack of sympathy, support, or understanding. Hence, seek that approval from your inner self; your conscience—it is your higher self.

- **Power vs. maneuver:** Instead of always thinking of using power in every situation, or becoming a power-conscious being, try to think in terms of a combination of power and multiple maneuvers. In any situation where one has to apply willpower and energy, use a combination of approaches, not just exerting yourself in one way because if you only think in terms of "hard work," or "energy/power exertion" then pretty soon you will experience burnout. Any long-term goals you set for yourself will go out of the window. To take care of the little and big details of life daily, and not feel irritated by the demands of balancing profession with personal, think of "flow," "combinations," "steps," "one thing at a time," and "a flow of energy and power descending into practical matters"—right from making one's bed, cooking a nice meal, to going for a 9-5 job, or sending out an email that is detail-oriented.

## WHAT'S POSSIBLE WITH THE RIGHT RELATION BETWEEN FREEDOM AND WILLPOWER

### *Extraordinary Solutions and Insights*

- **The maturity to collaborate** and come up with the best outcomes.
- **Unimaginable solutions/insights** that are undeniably the answers to complex issues.
- **Turning blocks into opportunities:** turning disfavor from others/clients/family members into wins, bonding, and collaborations.

### *Freedom vs. Being Bound by Responsibility*

- "With great power comes great responsibility"—famous lines quoted in the *Spiderman* movies.
- With great responsibility, freedom (in one sense) gets sacrificed. The good of others, duty toward others

and their welfare, become the overarching goal and priority in life.

- Non-attachment in the heart is also freedom.
- However, freedom is felt, in a sense, when you are a good leader if you discipline yourself well to meet all the demands on your time and energy. It is based on how much are you in control of your reactions/responses/functions. "Discipline is freedom," as Jocko Willink, the ex-Navy SEAL once said. Freedom is in disciplining yourself such that your commitments get fulfilled even with surmounting challenges. The exercise of freedom changes difficulties into smooth paths.
- The spirit of a true leader, a person such as an athlete, a NAVY seal, a fighter/soldier, or one who is out there serving bravely in the cold light of the day is one of responsible freedom—freedom that isn't misused, but one that sets an example for others and is transparent.

## CONCLUSION

Understanding freedom and willpower and their relationship is very crucial for those entering into greater responsibilities of leadership, or those wanting to execute their life's decisions like true leaders. Everyone is a leader in a way—they just don't know it. When we start to think and apply these pearls of wisdom related to constructive willpower and the corresponding relationship we need with freedom, we see that leadership becomes a very fruitful and successful endeavor—not a cause for burden, but rather, one that is a cause for great happiness.

# CONCLUSION

To conclude, military-style leadership is a life-transforming discipline. In this book, I have demonstrated the practicality and applicability of leadership principles to everyday life, both personal and professional. When you apply the tenets in this book, every day of your life will start to change and escalate into higher levels of understanding and success.

The power and knowledge behind every wise leader's words and actions have been a major force that brought success historically to countries, communities, groups, and individuals—it didn't matter what background or challenges these people came from. They became leaders in the course of their life. No one is born a leader, even if born into a family of monarchs. Leadership is an art that needs to be learned, studied, and applied.

The following is a final suggestion for the exercise of leadership principles. I wish you all the best with your leadership practice!

## SELF ASSESSMENT EXERCISE

### *Have a Basket of Choices to Exercise Freedom and Responsibility in a Smart Way*

You can ask yourself the following questions (you can have them written on flash cards separately and stored in a little workspace/desk basket) when a challenge comes up:

- Am I going to deal with this challenge or situation with the use of willpower?
- Am I going to understand this situation or challenge in a deeper way by first calming my heart and perception?
- Do I need to think about it from all different angles to understand it intellectually—all the possible details/concerns/consequences/effects on my life or where a possible decision can lead me?
- Do I need to change something in the level of energy in my body? The quality of how I feel about myself? Do I need to refresh my energy through exercise, a shower, sleep, or change to be able to handle this situation or come up with a solution?
- Do I need to communicate with someone and consciously be a medium for change and understanding to come about?
- Do I need to take responsibility for this situation in some way, a responsibility which I am currently shirking? If yes, do I need to apply a combination of the above techniques (willpower, feeling, intellect, body, communication) to deal with this challenge?

- If I am bothered by how I feel due to this challenge, how can I rid myself of this energy? And how do I purify/free/release myself from it? And is that all that's needed?

# ABOUT THE AUTHOR

1st Lieutenant Simpson is a dedicated and accomplished officer in the Texas State Guard, with a passion for leadership, education, and mentorship. Over the past three years, Lt. Simpson has served as a beacon of inspiration, leading, teaching, coaching, and mentorship to the numerous students who have passed through the training center he is a part of.

Lt. Simpson's commitment to excellence in education and training has not gone unnoticed, as he has been the recipient of multiple accolades for his outstanding achievements. His leadership style is characterized by a unique blend of discipline, compassion, service, and a relentless pursuit of excellence. Under his guidance, countless individuals have not only gained valuable skills and knowledge, but have also been instilled with a strong sense of duty and commitment to service.

A true advocate for personal and professional development, Lt. Simpson's ability to connect with his students on a personal level has fostered a supportive learning environment and has empowered individuals to reach their full potential. His leadership philosophy revolves around the belief that investing in others is the key to building a resilient and capable force.

As a seasoned officer, educator, and mentor, Lt. Simpson continues to make significant contributions to the Texas State Guard, leaving an indelible mark on those fortunate enough to have been under his instruction. His unwavering dedication to the principles of leadership, education, and mentorship serves as an inspiration to both his peers and the next generation of leaders within the organization.